A Day of Bear-y Big Adventures

Written by
Marydell Potter and Justin Potter

Original illustrations created by Marydell Potter with the assistance of AI technology.

Published by Marydell Potter

Marydellpotter@gmail.com

ISBN: 9798334799103

First Edition

To my son, Justin,

You are hard-working, tender-hearted, loving, and so kind. You fill my heart to overflowing with joy and pride. It was so much fun writing this book with you! I love being your mommy bear, my sweet little cub.

With all my love for forever, Mommy

A Day of Bear-y Big Adventures

In a cozy cave nestled behind a sparkling waterfall, there lived a loving bear family. Momma bear Merdel, Daddy bear Jumbo, and their playful cubs, Aaron and his sister Bella, enjoyed the warmth and comfort of their cave throughout the winter.

As the days grew warmer, tiny drops of spring rain trickled down the waterfall, and into the cave gently waking the bear family from their long slumber.

Aaron was the first to stir. He peeked out from the cave and felt the fresh spring air. "Momma, Daddy,

Bella, wake up! It's our family adventure day!" he exclaimed with excitement.

Merdel, Jumbo, and Bella stretched and yawned, smiling at the eager cub. "Let's start our adventure by getting some fresh water from the creek," suggested Merdel.

The family set off through the forest, marvelling at the bright green leaves and blooming flowers. The air was filled with the sweet scent of blossoms and the chirping of birds.

Aaron and Bella ran ahead, chasing butterflies and picking wildflowers.

When they reached the creek, Aaron leaned over to take a drink. Suddenly, he slipped and fell into the water with a splash.

"Aaron!" Merdel called out, but Aaron was a good swimmer. He swam right into a fish, grabbed it with his paws, and tossed it onto the shore. "I caught my first fish!" Aaron shouted, delighted.

Jumbo picked up the fish and said, "Great job, Aaron!" Merdel chuckled, "I said drink the water, not wear it!" Bella teased saying, "He needed a bath anyway!"

"Let's have a picnic by the creek," suggested Jumbo. They spread out a blanket and enjoyed their meal together.

Merdel watched her children and husband, feeling grateful for the simple joys of family life.

After their picnic, Aaron and Bella wanted to play hide and seek. "Daddy, you're it!" they declared.

Merdel, Aaron, and Bella went to hide, with Aaron climbing up a tree and Bella finding a spot behind

some bushes.

Jumbo snuck up behind Merdel and gently tapped her on the shoulder, making her jump and shriek. Aaron laughed so loudly that he gave away his hiding spot. When the laughter subsided, Merdel noticed how high Aaron had climbed. "Be careful, Aaron!" she said, worried.

Aaron felt a little scared but looked at his dad, who smiled and said, "You've got this, son. You're a strong, brave young bear." Encouraged by his dad's words, Aaron slowly and carefully climbed down the tree. When he reached the ground, Jumbo reached out and said, "Got you!" as he gently tagged Aaron.

"Dad, that's not fair!" Aaron giggled, squirming away. "But I found you and I tagged you, it totally counts!" Daddy said playfully. They all laughed so hard that they started snorting, their laughter echoing through the forest.

"Let's go see if there are any berries," Bella suggested, eager for the next adventure. They walked through the forest, following a winding path that led them through tall trees and over a gentle hill.

As they crested the hill, they saw a valley filled with glistening berries. The sight was magical, with the sun casting a golden glow over the bushes.

Aaron and Bella raced down the hill, eager to start picking. They quickly plucked the ripest berries and popped handfuls into their mouths, savouring the sweet, juicy flavour.

"Let's make berry crowns!" Bella suggested, weaving together stems and leaves. Aaron and Bella worked together, creating beautiful berry crowns adorned with red and purple berries. They placed the crowns on their heads, giggling at their creations. "All hail Prince Aaron and Princess Bella of the Berry Patch!" Aaron declared, bowing dramatically.

Merdel and Jumbo laughed. "Well, I guess that makes us the King and Queen of the Berry Patch," Jumbo said, placing a berry crown on Merdel's head.

Merdel, who loved taking pictures of everything, pulled out her camera. "Let's take a royal family selfie!" she said, gathering everyone together.

They all posed, crowns on their heads, and Merdel handed the cell phone to Dad to take the picture. Dad grumbled a bit teasingly, but in the end captured the joyful moment.

After taking the picture, the bear family continued their walk. As they strolled through the forest, Aaron suddenly stopped and sniffed the air. "Do you smell that?" he asked. "It smells sweet, like honey!" Merdel sniffed the air too and nodded. "I think you're right, Aaron. Let's follow the scent and see where it leads us."

The family followed the sweet smell deeper into the forest. Soon, they came upon a large tree with a hollow in its trunk. Inside the hollow, they saw a beehive dripping with golden honey. Bella's eyes widened with excitement. "Look at all that honey! Can we take some, Momma?"

Merdel smiled and nodded. "Let's be gentle and respectful of the bees. We'll take just enough for a treat."

Jumbo carefully reached into the hollow and scooped out some honeycomb, handing it to Aaron and Bella. They each took a bite and their faces lit up with delight. "It's so sweet and delicious!" Aaron exclaimed.

Merdel and Jumbo shared a piece of honeycomb as well, savouring the rich, sweet flavour. "This is a wonderful treat," Merdel said. "Let's thank God for this unexpected blessing in our day." With their honey treat in hand, the bear family continued their adventure, enjoying the sweetness and marvelling at the wonders of the forest.

As they continued their walk, Bella noticed something shiny on the ground. "Look! What's that?" she exclaimed, pointing to a small, glimmering object partially buried in the dirt.

Aaron carefully dug around the object and pulled out an old, dusty lantern. "It looks like a lantern from a long time ago," he said, examining it. "I wonder if it still works."

Merdel suggested, "Let's see if we can find some fireflies to put inside. They might make it glow again!"

Aaron and Bella excitedly agreed. They gently caught several fireflies and placed them inside the lantern.

To their amazement, the lantern began to glow softly, illuminating their path. "This is magical!" Bella said,

her eyes wide with wonder.

As the sun set, they made their way back to their cave, guided by the gentle glow of the firefly lantern.

Once they made it back home, they decided they would enjoy the warm evening and watch the stars and moon. Sitting on a log outside, they looked up at the moon. "The moon shines bright tonight," Merdel said, holding Aaron and Bella close. Aaron snuggled into his parents' laps, feeling tired and happy.

He looked at the moon and his family and whispered, "Just like your love, Momma." With a contented sigh, he drifted off to sleep, knowing he was loved and safe.

As Merdel and Jumbo sat holding their children in their arms as they slept, their worries drifted far away, and their hearts filled with endless love for their children and each other. This moment was perfect and peaceful, and they both silently thanked God for each other and their children. Then, with gentle care, they carried them off to bed.

The End

Manufactured by Amazon.ca
Bolton, ON